How to write what you want to say ... in science

a guide for those who know what they want to say but can't find the words

Malcolm Carter, Lyn Carter
and Patricia Hipwell

Count on Numeracy

logonliteracy

First published 2016

National Library of Australia Cataloguing-in-Publication entry

Creator:	Carter, Malcolm, author.
Title:	How to write what you want to say ... in science : a guide for those who know what they want to say but can't find the words / Malcolm Carter, Lyn Carter and Patricia Hipwell.
ISBN:	9781925236903 (paperback), 9781925522563 (ebook)
Subjects:	Science–Methodology. Communication in science. Technical writing.
Other Creators/Contributors:	Carter, Lyn, author. Hipwell, Patricia, author.
Dewey Number:	808.0666

Typeset in Delicious 10 pt.

Text and cover design: **Boolarong Press**

Image of *Pencil-pusher* by Zsuzsanna Kilian

Note: Text examples of the writing skill in scientific have been created to demonstrate that skill. Possible inaccuracies and out-of-date information in these texts are acknowledged by the authors and do not detract from the validity of their inclusion.

Published by Boolarong Press, Salisbury, Brisbane, Australia.

Printed and bound by Watson Ferguson & Company, Salisbury, Brisbane, Australia.

contents

dedication

'If I have seen further than others, it is by standing upon the shoulders of giants.' (Sir Isaac Newton)

This book is dedicated to the 'giants' of the scientific world, with thanks for allowing us all to stand on their shoulders.

introduction

This guide, written by Malcolm and Lyn Carter of Count on Numeracy and Patricia Hipwell of logonliteracy, provides students with the language they need to write for a variety of purposes in science. It aims to provide inexperienced writers with a starting point to say what they want to say using language that mature writers use.

Most of the book is set out in a double-page format:

- The first page describes the skill, gives some tips for students, and provides examples of sentence starters commonly used in that form of writing.
- The second page provides words that are commonly used in that form of writing and gives an example of the skill in a short text.

At the end of the book there are several sections providing more general information to improve the sophistication of writing and to meet the expectations of scientific texts.

How to write what you want to say ... in science is a guide for those who know what they want to say but can't find the words. It provides a unique tool for improving scientific writing. It suits inexperienced writers in science from the middle years of schooling to tertiary level.

This book is the sixth in a series and takes a similar approach to:

How to write what you want to say by Patricia Hipwell

How to write what you want to say ... in mathematics by Lyn Carter and Patricia Hipwell

How to write what you want to say ... in the primary years by Catherine Black and Patricia Hipwell

How to write what you want to say ... in business by Lyn Carter and Patricia Hipwell

How to write what you want to say ... at university by Patricia Hipwell and Lyn Carter

the nature of scientific writing

The aim of this book is to improve the sophistication of the writing that accompanies or supports scientific experiments, investigations and arguments.

Scientific writing aims to offer solutions based on theory and observations. There are two important aspects to writing correctly in the sciences: the science must be valid and the writing must be grammatically correct.

Scientific writing contains some common features. It

- conveys factual information
- assumes an educated audience
- has a formal, academic tone
- often uses the past tense and passive voice
- avoids personal pronouns, contractions and clichés (see pages 48 and 49)
- is impartial (avoids bias and opinion)
- includes evidence, in the form of observations, measurements, citations and references
- uses scientific terms
- includes symbols, tables and visual images
- is a precise and concise form of communication.

Scientific method

Scientific method is a well-established approach to asking and answering questions about the natural world by observation and experimentation. It involves

- posing a question
- undertaking background research in order to make predictions
- constructing a hypothesis based on predictions
- testing the hypothesis by experimentation
- analysing the experimental results
- drawing conclusions
- reporting.

The first part of this book demonstrates the forms of writing used to describe these processes. These sections can be combined to form a comprehensive scientific report.

key terms and ideas defined

form of writing	the type or style of text to be produced, for example, deducing, hypothesising
purpose	the use or reason for this form of writing
things to know	important information about the form of writing
sentence starters	the opening clause of the sentence; these sentence starters are shown in bold in the examples of each form of writing
useful scientific vocabulary	some suggested language that is characteristic of, or commonly used in, the form of writing; this useful scientific vocabulary is underlined in the examples of each form of writing
citations	links to documents that provide the source of the information used (see pages 46 and 47)
key task word glossary	words used in questions to establish what is required in the answer, and give a clear purpose for the type of writing required (see pages 55 to 59)
scientific glossary	definitions of scientific words used in this book (see pages 60 to 63)

introducing

purpose

beginning a text by describing what it is about

things to know

Introductions can include why the experiment is important, aims/objectives, key definitions, important issues, and what follows.

The introduction is often one of the last sections to be written.

sentence starters

It can be argued/has been suggested that ...

A common view is that ...

There are two main views about ...

The background to this issue was ...

The aim/objective of this experiment/study/investigation was ...

The issue was important because ...

The investigation/experiment is interesting/significant/useful because ...

Before continuing, it is necessary to explain the meaning of some key terms.

The important concepts in this experiment were ...

The scientific term ..., which means ..., should not be confused with the everyday use of the word, meaning ...

This report contains ... sections, as follows: ...

An outline of this report is as follows: ...

useful scientific vocabulary

aimed/aim	examined	investigated/investigation	purpose
commonly	explored	is in the third section	relationship
comprised	follows/following	issues	significant/significance
concept	goal	link	the final section
connection	important/importance	mattered/matters	the next section
data	included	meaning	this section
defined/definition	involved/involving	method	to determine
essential	intended/intention	objective	to find

example

It can be argued that steel is the most important metal in the world because it is the most widely used. Steel is an essential part of the construction of buildings, motor vehicles, appliances and infrastructure such as roads and railways. Most large modern structures, such as stadiums, skyscrapers, bridges and airports, are supported by a steel skeleton. Even those made of concrete use steel for reinforcement. It is essential that steel is able to withstand corrosion.

The aim of this experiment was two-fold: (a) to determine the conditions that promote the corrosion of steel; and (b) to find out how corrosion can be prevented or reduced.

The important concepts in this experiment were steel and corrosion. Steels are alloys of iron (Fe) and other elements, primarily carbon (C), widely used because of their high tensile strengths and low costs. Corrosion is defined as a natural process, involving the destruction of materials (usually metals or alloys) by the surrounding environment through chemical and electrochemical changes*. In the case of iron and steel, corrosion is commonly called rusting.

This experimental **report contains five sections.** Following this introduction, some background research is presented, leading to the development of six hypotheses about the rusting of steel. The second section on experimental process describes the experimental design, procedures, and method, followed by a third section that presents the observed data. In the discussion section, data are analysed and deductions made. The report ends with recommendations to prevent the corrosion of steel, and a conclusion.

**A citation providing evidence for the assertion would normally be included here (see pages 46 and 47 on how to do this).*

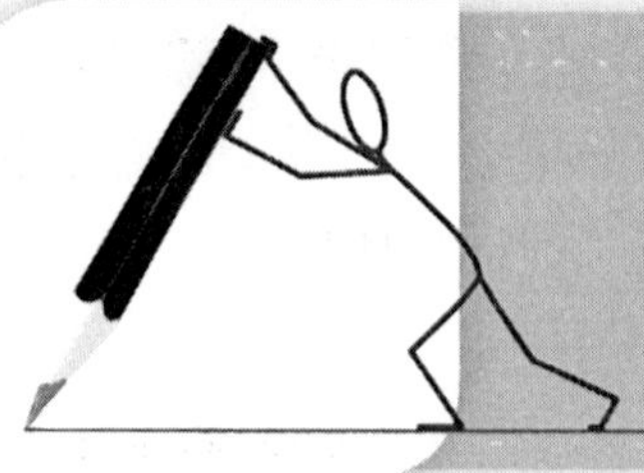

researching the background

purpose

summarising and analysing the sources of information relevant to the subject under investigation

things to know

Background research gives basic information about a subject. It can provide (a) a broad overview of the subject, (b) definitions of important words and ideas, (c) identification of key issues and processes, (d) an understanding of the theory, (e) names of people who are authorities in the subject, (f) significant dates and events, (g) key words that can be used to search for further information, and (h) bibliographies of additional resources. Background research should use reputable, peer-reviewed sources (see glossary). A description of research must include references to the source of the information.

sentence starters

A substantial body of literature is relevant to a study of … ‹*cite some key examples*›.

The review of literature, detailed below, revealed that …

The background research covered …‹*number*› areas …

The research/theory proposes/suggests that …

This experiment/report/study focuses on …

The scientific theory/theories relevant to this investigation are …

The theory was developed by … ‹*name(s), date(s)*›, who proposed that …

A consequence of the theory is that …

The history of this topic is …

… is/has already been defined as …‹*meaning*› ‹*source*›

The term has several meanings. In this study/experiment it is used to refer to …

The theory relevant to this investigation/experiment is …

(Author 1, date) stated … and this directly supported the findings of (author 2, date), who noted …

This topic draws on the work of … in …, who found that …

Whilst some argue that …, these views are invalid because …

… refers to …

In the case of …

This means that …

The original theory was modified by … to …

useful scientific vocabulary

background	important	overview	significant
bibliography	issues	reliable/reliably	source
cited/citation	involved/involving	research	summary/summarised
defined/definition	key	process	theory
focus/focuses	list of references	scientific literature	valid/invalid
found/finding	meaning	searched	

example

This experiment focuses on iron (Fe) and an alloy of iron, steel. An alloy is a metal made by combining two or more metallic elements, especially to give greater strength or resistance to corrosion. Carbon (C) is frequently included in steel to act as a hardening agent that prevents ions movements that would otherwise occur in the crystal lattices of Fe atoms. Steels are widely used because of their high tensile strengths and low costs*.

Corrosion **has already been defined as** a natural process, involving the destruction of metals or alloys (usually) by the surrounding environment. Corrosion **theory proposes that, in the case of** steel, it is an electrochemical process requiring the simultaneous presence of moisture (water) and oxygen. The iron in the steel is oxidised to produce hydrated iron oxide (rust) that forms on the surface of the steel*. Further, when two different metals come into contact, any corrosion occurs on the surface of the more reactive metal*.

There are many adverse consequences of corrosion. They include weakening of the steel leading to failure of the structure it supports; the need to replace the corroded steel; reduced value of structures and goods; contamination of substances coming into contact with the rust; loss of essential surface properties such as smoothness, conductivity, or reflectivity; mechanical damage; and blockage of pipes*.

A consequence of the theory of corrosion is that it can be prevented by ensuring that the steel does not come into contact with agents of corrosion, that is water and/or oxygen. It can be slowed by removing those things that accelerate corrosion such as salt water, heat and contact with a different type of metal. On the other hand, since corrosion occurs on contact between the metal and the agents of corrosion, large surface areas increase the rate of corrosion*.

**A citation providing evidence for these assertions would normally be included here* *(see pages 46 and 47 on how to do this).*

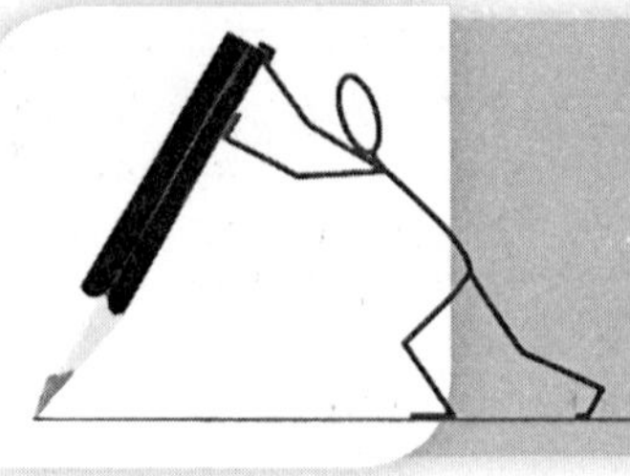

hypothesising

purpose

proposing a scientific explanation for, or predicting the outcome of, a process or event

things to know

A scientific hypothesis is a testable statement proposing how two or more variables might be related. It provides a basis for a scientific experiment. It can be a cause and effect statement (if ... then) or a prediction.

Hypotheses are usually based on observations of the environment. They usually seek to confirm or negate (falsify) a scientific theory. They provide a context for the analysis and discussion of the experimental findings.

A hypothesis based on cause and effect is usually written in present tense. If the hypothesis is a prediction, it is written in future tense.

sentence starters

... ‹*cause*› will lead to ... ‹*effect*›.

If ...‹*cause*› then ...‹*effect*›.

It was hypothesised that ...

Observations of ... suggested that ...

Some of these/These observations were ...

Taking into account/after considering/the research into ..., ...‹*number*› further hypotheses were proposed: ...

This led to the following hypothesis/hypotheses to be tested by this experiment: ...

useful scientific vocabulary

cause	hypothesis (singular)/ hypotheses (plural)	occur	suggest(s) that
effect	if ... then	proposed/proposal	theory
environment	lead/led to	research into	variable
experiment/ experimentation	observe/observation	scientific	will

example

Observations of the rusting of metals include:

- garden tools that have been oiled do not rust as quickly as tools that have not been oiled;
- cars in coastal environments rust more quickly than cars in desert environments;
- rusting occurs when a brass handle is attached to a steel door frame; and
- more rust is evident at sharp metal corners than on smooth surfaces.

Some of these observations were confirmed by **research into** corrosion theory, **which proposes that** heat, water, salt water and contact with other metals either cause or increase the rate of corrosion. **They led to six hypotheses to be tested by this experiment:**

1. exposure to water and air **will lead to** corrosion;
2. exposure to salt water **will lead to** increased corrosion rates;
3. coating the surface **will lead to** reduced corrosion rates
4. surfaces stressed by sharp bends **will lead to** increased corrosion rates; and
5. contact with other types of metals **will lead to** changes in the rate of corrosion.

After considering the research into corrosion theory, a **further hypothesis was proposed**:

6. increased surface area **will lead to** an increased rate of corrosion.

designing the experiment

purpose

explaining the reasons for the experimental processes used to test the hypothesis/ hypotheses

things to know

This style of writing focuses on ***why*** *things were done. It differs from describing experimental method or procedure, which focuses on* ***how*** *they were done.*

A controlled experiment usually has several parts. In one part, there is no treatment or change in any of the experimental variables (called the control or control group). In the remainder of the experiment, each variable is changed or treated, one at a time, with all other conditions remaining constant. Experimental controls eliminate other possible explanations of experimental results. See also the definition of the different types of variables in the glossary.

The design of an experiment should include consideration of risk and hazards, taking into account information on Material Safety Data Sheets (MSDS), and the necessary safety precautions.

A design may need to be modified during the course of an investigation, if difficulties are encountered.

sentence starters

Based on the hypothesis/hypotheses, the conditions to be investigated in this experiment involved ...

It was decided to ... because ...

The method chosen was ... because ...

The changes were controlled by ...

The experimental control was ...

The intention was ...

This study required an experimental design that ...

These conditions were replicated in the laboratory by ...

useful scientific vocabulary

category/categories	experiment	hypothesis/ hypotheses	required/requirement
condition(s)	experimental control	individually	tested/testable
control group	experimental design	investigated/ investigation	treated/treatment
controlled experiment	experimental variable		types

example

Based on the hypotheses, the conditions to be investigated in this experiment involved:

1. exposure to air and/or water;
2. exposure to salt water;
3. coated surfaces;
4. stressed surfaces;
5. contact with other types of metals; and
6. large surface area (relative to mass).

Inspection of this list showed that the experimental variables were of two types:

A. those related to the nature of the metal, its surface, or contact with other metals; and

B. those related to the environment in which the metal was placed.

The intention was for each metal type to be tested in each environmental condition. Having two variable types **required an experimental design** that involved the use of two experimental controls. The experimental design is summarised in Table 1.

TABLE 1. EXPERIMENTAL CONTROLS AND VARIABLES

Variable Type A: Nature of the Metal		Variable Type B: Environment	
Control	*Steel nail*	*Control*	*Water with air removed*
Coated surface	Steel wool	Water (H_2O)	Tap water
Stressed surface	Sharply bent nail	Air	Air
Large surface area	Oiled nail	Water (H_2O) containing salt (NaCl)	Tap water and NaCl
Contact with other metals	Contact with Cu		
	Contact with Mg		

For simplicity, **these conditions were replicated in the laboratory by** a series of test tube experiments. One variable was changed in each test tube. This required a matrix design, involving 24 (6 x 4) test tubes.

describing procedures

purpose

giving a detailed account of the process(es) of conducting an experiment

things to know

This style of writing focuses on ***how*** *things were done.*

A diagram can be a useful addition to illustrate what is happening.

sentence starters

The equipment was prepared by/as follows: ...

The following method was used to investigate ...

The solution/samples were treated/heated/mixed ...

... was/were placed in ...

This was followed by ...

In the next stage of the (experiment), ...

The second/next step/process involved ...

After ... was completed/prepared, ...

The final part of the process included ...

On completion, ...

The appearance of the samples was observed daily over a period of ...

... were set up as shown in Table ‹*number*›.

Figure ‹*number*› illustrates the set-up of the apparatus ...

..., illustrated in Figure ‹*number*›, ...

useful scientific vocabulary

added	finally	planned	solution
after	following/followed by	preceded	stage
began/beginning	initially	preparation/prepared	started (with)
commenced	investigated/investigation	procedure	step
concluded	measurement/measured	process	succession
datum (singular)/ data (plural)	method	progressed/progression	tested
decanted	mixture	recorded	treated/untreated
equipment	observed/observation	sample	washed
experiment	order	sequence	

example

To investigate the corrosion of steel, 24 test tube experiments were conducted. **The equipment was prepared as follows:**

1. 50 steel nails were washed in detergent (to remove any adhering oils), dried, and then divided into five groups of 10 and treated in the following manner:
   a. no further treatment
   b. bent sharply
   c. coated in oil
   d. wound with magnesium (Mg) ribbon
   e. wound with copper (Cu) wire.
2. Three sets of six washed test tubes (18 test tubes in all) were prepared, with each set respectively containing:
   a. tap water, boiled for at least five minutes to remove the air from the water, cooled, and then a layer of oil added to the surface to prevent air dissolving back into the water
   b. tap water
   c. tap water with salt (NaCl) added.
3. The remaining six test tubes were washed and dried.
4. The steel wool was untreated.

The 24 test tubes **were set up** and labelled **as shown in Table 2.**

TABLE 2. PREPARATION OF TEST TUBES

	Boiled tap water, with oil	Tap water	Tap water and NaCl	Air
2 untreated steel nails				
2 bent nails				
2 oiled nails				
Steel wool				
2 nails wound in Cu wire				
2 nails wound with Mg ribbon				

The test tubes were kept at room temperature. **The appearance of the samples was observed** at approximately 1.00 pm **daily over a period of** seven days.

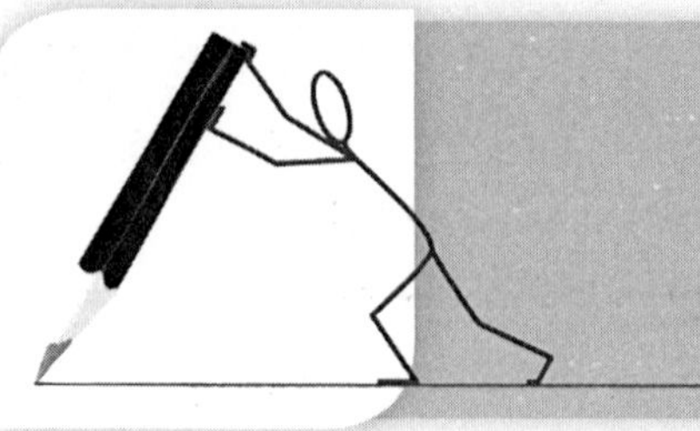

observing

purpose

describing the process of collecting information (data), involving the use of the senses and scientific equipment, and recording these data

things to know

Additional information about observations and how to record them is given in the section on scientific data on pages 44 and 45.

Data collected in an experiment should be recorded in an organised manner, often using tables, so that others can review the data easily.

The substitutes for showed that on page 51 may be useful.

sentence starters

The solution/sample/reaction was observed ...

The colour/smell/appearance/sound/taste of ... was recorded.

The number of ... was counted and recorded in ...

... was measured using ..., with the results recorded in ...

The experimental results/data were recorded in ...

... was/were measured/recorded.

The information was tabulated/recorded in Table ‹*number*›.

The data/results were tabulated/recorded in Table ‹*number*›.

The daily observations were tabulated.

Table/Figure ‹*number*› summarises the observations/results.

..., shown in Table/Figure ‹*number*›, ...

The information was detailed/summarised/presented in ...

useful scientific vocabulary

accurate/accuracy	extent	occur/occurrence	sample
appearance	frequency	per second/minute/ hour/day	smell
counted	measurement/measured	precise/precision	table/tabulated
colour	noted/noting	reacted/reaction	tally/tallied
daily	observed/observation	recorded	temperature
datum (singular)/ data (plural)		results/resulted	

example

The appearance of the steel samples **was observed and recorded** over seven days, particularly noting the occurrence and extent of rusting. **These observations were tabulated** (see Table 3).

TABLE 3. CORROSION EXPERIMENT RESULTS

Test tube contents	Day	Room temperature			
		Boiled water	Tap water	Water and NaCl	Air
Untreated steel nails	Day 1				
	Day 2				
	Day 3				
	Day 4				
	Day 5				
	Day 6				
	Day 7				
Bent steel nails	Day 1				
	Day 2				
	Day 3				
	Day 4				
	Day 5				
	Day 6				
	Day 7				

Data are entered in these cells

[The table continues with another 28 rows for the other four types of samples.]

analysing

purpose

interpreting logically the meaning of experimental results to obtain useful information for predicting outcomes, formulating conclusions or supporting decisions

things to know

Analysis is often described as the process of examining the parts of something in detail and discussing or interpreting the relationship of the parts to each other and to the whole. In the context of a scientific experiment, it involves a detailed examination of the experimental results.

Both the process of analysis and the interpretation of the data should be described.

Graphs and calculations (for example, the mean) may be used to assist in the analysis of data collected in an experiment.

sentence starters

The data in Table ‹*number*› were analysed by ...

Some of the data collected in this experiment were inaccurate because ...

Some observations/data were excluded because ...

This aberrant result occurred because of errors in experimental procedure.

This result was inconsistent with ...

The data were converted from ... to .../analysed by ...

The mean/median/mode of ... was calculated/determined to be ...

This means that/allowed/enabled ...

It was assumed/concluded that ...

The extent of ... was judged/determined by ...

The main similarities/differences in the data were ...

The graph/table/result showed/revealed that ...

The data reveal/revealed the following trends: ...

The data revealed a strong connection between ...

The ... increased/declined as ... increased/decreased.

There was an inverse relationship between ... and ...

The relationship between ... and ... was ...

On the basis of this experiment ...

useful scientific vocabulary

aberrant	contradicted	extrapolated	results
accompanied (by)	converted	facts/factual/factually	showed that
analysed/analysis	datum (singular)/data (plural)	graphed/graph/ graphically	strength
associated (with)	demonstrated/ demonstration	however	suggested that
calculated/calculation	estimated	information	supported by
changed/increased/ decreased/etc	evaluated	interpolated	tabulated/table
compared/comparison	evidence	interpreted/interpretation	weakness
conclusive/conclusively	experimental error	ranked/ranking	whereas
consisted of	experimenter bias	reasoned/reasoning	which was/allowed/gave
	extent	refuted	

example

The data in Table 3 **were analysed by comparing** (a) the different treatments of steel (shown in rows), and (b) the different conditions that the steel was exposed to (shown in columns). **The** extent **of corrosion was judged by** the amount of rust and the colour of the liquid.

None of the metals corroded in air or boiled water. In both salt and tap water the steel wool and nails with Cu were the most corroded, with the steel wool corroding sooner. In the water with added NaCl, corrosion was detected on the bent nails, the untreated nails and one of the oiled nails, whereas no corrosion was detected on the other oiled nails and nails with Mg. In tap water the bent and the untreated nails corroded slightly. In both cases, the corrosion on the bent nails was detected earlier than on the untreated nails. **It was concluded that** the steel wool corroded most easily, followed by the nails with Cu and then the bent nails. The untreated nails were ranked fourth and, **on the basis of this experiment**, the oiled nails fifth. The nails with Mg reacted the least.

The steel samples in boiled water and air showed no signs of corrosion. Some of the metals corroded in water with and without added NaCl, but in each case, it was more extensive in water with NaCl added. **It was concluded that** water containing air and NaCl causes corrosion more rapidly than water containing air without added NaCl. However, removing either air (in the case of boiled water) or water seemed to be sufficient to prevent corrosion.

Rust was detected on a small section of one of the oiled nails in the water with added NaCl. **This result was inconsistent with** the other results in this experiment and also with the results of similar experiments conducted elsewhere in the class. It is suggested that **this aberrant result occurred** because one of the nails was not oiled thoroughly, that is, **because of errors in experimental procedure**.

reasoning deductively

purpose

using logical thinking to arrive at a conclusion from known or assumed fact(s)

things to know

Deductive reasoning is 'top down' that is; it starts with a general statement, or hypothesis, makes testable predictions based on the hypothesis, gathers data through observation and/or experimentation to test the predictions, and finally develops theories that are consistent with the data. For example, given the hypothesis that objects with different masses fall at the same rate, the testable prediction is that two objects with the same size and shape, but different masses, when dropped from a height will reach the ground at the same time. An experiment is designed to determine if the prediction is true. If the two objects reach the ground at the same time, the hypothesis is accepted; otherwise, it is rejected.

Past tense is used to discuss results, but present tense is used to describe theory, conclusions and propositions.

sentence starters

In this experiment ... occurred/did not occur if/when ...

This suggested that ... has an important role in ...

These results showed that ...

This finding supported the hypothesis/proposition that ...

... is linked to ...

... increased/decreased the likelihood of ...

It can be concluded that ...

If ... then ...

Based on the research, ...

useful scientific vocabulary

argued/argument	finding	premise	rigour/rigorous
accepted	for example	probability	suggested
assumed/ assumption	for instance	proposition	supported
concluded/ conclusion	likelihood	rejected	testable
deduced/ deduction	occur/occurred	required/ requirement	therefore
fact	otherwise	resulted/results	

example

In this experiment corrosion **did not occur** in air alone or in water where the air had been removed by boiling. Further, thoroughly coating the surface of the steel with oil to prevent contact with air and water seemed to prevent corrosion. **These results demonstrated that** the presence of both air and water is required for steel to corrode.

The steel wool, with its large surface area, was the most corroded. **This finding supported the proposition that** the rate of corrosion **is linked to** the area of the surface exposed to water and air. Water, air and NaCl seemed to be a particularly corrosive combination. **This suggested that** NaCl **has an important role in increasing** the rate of corrosion. Putting stress on the steel, for example by deformation (bending), also **increased the likelihood of** corrosion.

Contact with the unreactive Cu promoted corrosion, whereas contact with the reactive Mg did not. **Based on the research, this suggested that** placing a reactive metal in contact with the steel may reduce corrosion of the steel.

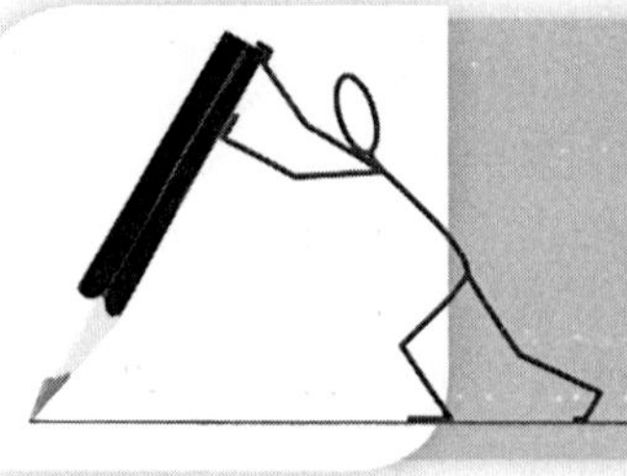

recommending

purpose

suggesting a course of action for consideration by others

things to know

A recommendation usually provides reasons (linked to the findings of the investigation) in favour of the suggestion.

Recommendations may also deal with safety issues.

sentence starters

It is recommended that ...

This experiment process has led to the conclusion that ..., and it is therefore recommended that ...

Based on the experimental findings/results, the following/... ‹*number*› recommendations are proposed: ...

After examining all the evidence, it is recommended that ...

It is, therefore, advisable to ...

The following recommendations, listed in order of priority, are proposed: ...

Based on the outcome of the experiment, the following recommendations can be made: ...

The following changes are recommended: ...

In light of the problem of ..., a suitable solution should include ...

To achieve its aims, the experiment needs to be modified to ...

The proposed recommendations, with a summary of the reasons for each, are listed below.

Further experiments are needed/recommended to ...

useful scientific vocabulary

achieved/ achievement	advocated	improved/ improvement	suggested/ suggestion
acted/action	benefited	proposed/proposal	strategy/strategies
advised/ advice	concluded/ conclusion	recommended/ recommendation	summarised
adopted			

example

Steel is an essential part of the construction of buildings, vehicles, appliances and community infrastructure. Most large modern structures are supported by a steel skeleton. Even those made of concrete use steel for reinforcement. It is essential that steel can withstand corrosion. The experimental results suggested several strategies that can be adopted, either individually or in combination, to reduce the rate of corrosion in steel. **Based on the experimental results, six recommendations are proposed.**

- Removal of air and/or water from the environment, where possible.
- Minimising contact with sea water and/or removal of salt after contact with the sea.
- Coating the surface of the steel with a substance that prevents contact with air and water (such as oil, plastic, paint), with regular maintenance or replacement of the coating.
- Minimising the exposed surface area.
- Reducing the stresses placed on the steel through deformation, for example by avoiding designs that require sharp folds in the steel.
- Using a "sacrificial" reactive metal in contact with the steel, if the sacrificial metal can be replaced more easily or cheaply than the steel structure.

The experiment also showed that rusting can occur rapidly in certain conditions. As the consequences of corrosion can be dire, **it is advisable to** develop regular procedures for the critical examination and maintenance of steel structures to ensure that they continue to be fit for purpose.

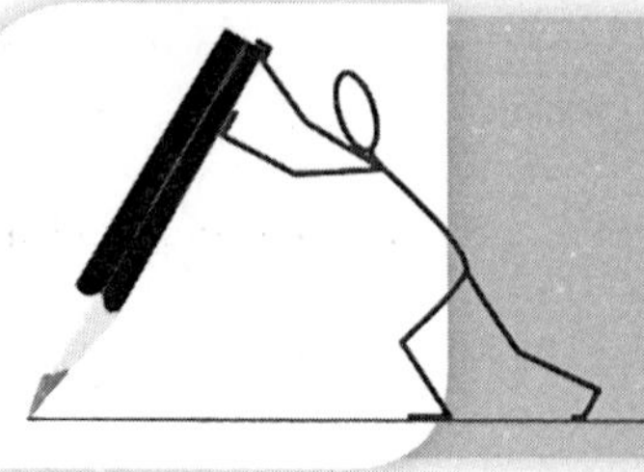

concluding

purpose

drawing together the main ideas and restating them in a succinct way

things to know

The conclusion of an experimental report may examine: the original hypotheses; the original aims to determine whether they were met; and the limitations of the experiment.

sentence starters

Thus, to conclude/in conclusion ...
It can be concluded that ...
To sum up/summarise, ...
In summary, ...
An examination of all the data allows the following conclusions to be drawn: ...
The experiment supports the conclusion that ...
It is not clear ...
An examination of the experimental evidence allows the following summary to be made: ...
... hypotheses were proposed to give effect to the aims of the experiment. Examining each of them in turn: ...
It is now possible to comment on the experimental hypotheses ...
A strength of this conclusion/approach is ...
The conclusions of this experiment/investigation are limited to ...
These conclusions could also/could not be applied/extended to ...
This experiment had several/the following limitations: ...
Given that the aim of this experiment was to ..., this report shows that this objective was partially/fully met.
The aims of the experiment could not be fully met because ...
The following unexpected outcomes occurred: ...
A further investigation/experiment could extend this work by ...
Further experiments would be required to ...
... might have been observed had the experiment ...
A more extensive experiment could/might have ...

useful scientific vocabulary

although	consequence/ consequently	goals	limited (to)/limitation
application	effect (of assumptions)	hypothesis/ hypotheses	outcome
assumed (that)	expected	impact	results
briefly	extended (to)/ extension	importance/important	significance/significant
clarified/clear	finally	in closing	summed (up)/ summarised/summary
concluded/conclusion	found/finding	inconclusive/ inconclusively	unexpected
			was/were

example

The aim of this experiment was two-fold: (a) to determine the conditions that promote the corrosion of steel; and (b) to find how corrosion can be prevented or reduced. **Six hypotheses were proposed to give effect to these aims**. The discussion showed that they were all confirmed. **To summarise,** exposure to water and air was necessary for steel to corrode. The following conditions increased the rate of corrosion: exposure to salt; larger surface area; deformation of the steel; and contact with a less reactive metal. Corrosion can be prevented or reduced by: thorough removal of salt after contact; coating of the steel surface to prevent contact with water and air; and the use of a "sacrificial" more reactive metal.

The experiment had several limitations. First, it could have tested a wider range of conditions in which steel might corrode, for example higher temperatures (to simulate tropical conditions), higher humidity, and weak acid (to simulate the effect of acid rain). A second limitation was that the duration of the experiment was limited to one week only. Corrosion in air might **have been observed had the experiment** been conducted over a longer period. Third, the experiment relied only on what was seen in the test tubes. **A more extensive experiment might have** tested the liquid in the test tubes for the presence of Fe^{2+} and Fe^{3+} ions. Finally, only one type of metal (steel alloy) and one type of salt (NaCl) were tested. **The conclusions about** the rusting of steel **cannot be extended to** other metals and/or salts without widening the experiment to include those other substances.

Steel is commonly used in building and construction, vehicles, tools and equipment, and community infrastructure. It is essential for the safety and durability of these structures and equipment that steel is used in ways that resist corrosion.

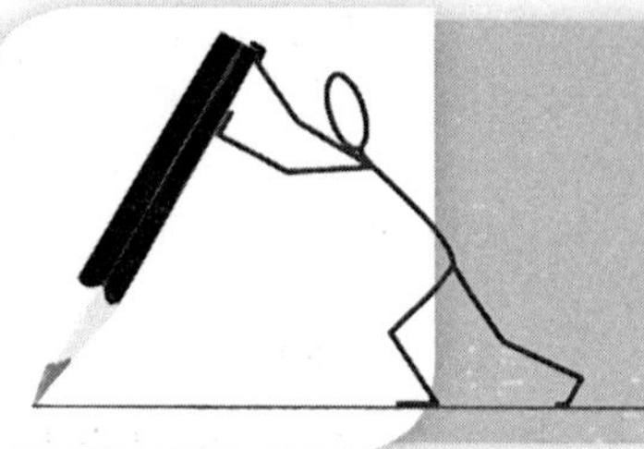

arguing/ persuading

purpose

presenting both sides of an argument to reach a conclusion (arguing); using logical and factual persuasive techniques to convince others that your opinion about something is the correct one (persuading)

things to know

In the sciences, an argument presents both sides of the case objectively and draws a conclusion based on the evidence. In a scientific argument, personal opinions should be introduced only if specifically requested.

Persuasion involves convincing the reader that one side of the argument is correct. Personal opinions and subjective statements may be used. Although persuasion is not a common form of scientific writing, it is often used by non-scientists to criticise scientific conclusions.

sentence starters

It is argued that ...
Opinion is divided on the issue of ...
There is a convincing argument/are several convincing arguments to support this point of view.
The issue of ... is controversial because ...
There has been much debate about ...
The main objection to these alternatives is ...
There is a compelling argument to ...
In spite of/Despite this ...
Those who disagree say that ...
The evidence points to ...
... has/have been vehemently opposed to ...
There is a great deal of evidence to support ..., not least of which is ...
The evidence that supports this argument is accurate/credible/reliable/unreliable/difficult to substantiate.
Whilst there are several convincing arguments that support this point of view, the balance of the argument is weighted in favour of ...
It would appear that the issue of ... is quite straightforward; however, closer inspection reveals ...
There are compelling arguments both in favour of and against ...

useful scientific vocabulary

alternative	convincing/ convincingly	limitation	refuted
agreed/agreement	counter-argument	on balance	strength
argued/argument	data	on the other hand	supported/supposition
case	debate	opinion	thought
claimed	demonstrated/ demonstration	persuaded/persuasion	unresolved
compelling	disagreed/ disagreement	point of view	weakness
conclusive/ conclusively	evidence	proved/proof	
contradicted	facts/factual	reasoned/reasoning	

example

During World War II 1554 ships were sunk*. All of these vessels contained fuel, and many carried explosives and toxic cargoes. They have now been in a corrosive environment for more than 70 years. It is likely that corrosion will release these dangerous and polluting substances into the marine environment. **It is argued that** the risk of environmental damage is serious and that preventative action should be investigated urgently. There is a need for action at both an international and a local level.

On the other hand, **those who disagree say that** many of these vessels are in deep or cold water. It would be difficult and expensive to reach them, and risky and challenging to remove or seal any dangerous substances and pollutants they contain. As many of the ships are in international waters, there is also the unresolved question as to who would pay for the clean-up. **There is a compelling argument that** these ships should be left untouched as memorials to those who died in them.

On balance, although **opinion is divided on the issue**, the cost of environmental damage through uncontrolled leakage of dangerous substances and pollutants will be high. It is likely to outweigh the cost of preventing leakages. Given the global nature of the problem, the United Nations should be the body to coordinate the action. Accordingly, the argument for taking urgent investigative action is more convincing.

**Citations providing the sources of the information and assertions in this example would normally be included (see pages 46 and 47 on how to do this).*

comparing

purpose

identifying the ways that two or more things are similar **and** different

things to know

A comparison is not a parallel description; that is, avoid writing about one thing and then writing about another. The best way to avoid a parallel description is to structure the text around the attributes/qualities/properties/features of the things being compared.

When planning a comparison, it can be helpful to sort your ideas using a Venn diagram (overlapping circles). Each circle represents the things being compared, with the overlapping section used to show the similarities, and the differences shown in the sections that do not overlap.

sentence starters

There are similarities and differences in ...

The elements of ... and ... will be compared.

A and B are both ...

In both cases ...,

There are several ways in which A and B are similar, including ...

The most striking similarity between A and B is ...

This is similar to ...

The similarities between ... and ... are more relevant than the differences.

Closer inspection reveals that, whilst A and B appear very similar, subtle differences exist.

... and ... have more in common than ... and ..., especially the fact that ...

... and ... are similar as they both show ...

Several differences exist in/between ...

The main/most important difference is ...

Obvious differences exist between A and B, particularly the fact that ...

This differs from ...

Specific differences exist between ... and ...

The similarities between A and B are insignificant when compared with their differences.

A comparison of ... and ... reveals noteworthy and highly significant differences.

The features of ... and ... are similar, whereas the features of ... and ... are different.

Just as ... is/are ..., so ... is/are ...

useful scientific vocabulary

aligned	both	dissimilar	more/less/fewer than
alike/like/unlike	but	diverse	nevertheless
also	by comparison	equal/equated	same
although	case	however	similar/similarity/ similarly
altered	changed	in contrast	situation
analogous	common to	instance	usually
another	compared with/ comparable/comparison	judged	whereas
assessed	differed (from)/different/ differences	matched	while/whilst

example

There are two principal kingdoms of living things: plants and animals. Cells are the basis of life in both kingdoms; however, **there are similarities and differences in** the nature of those cells.

Several differences exist in the structure of the two types of cell. Plant cells tend to be larger and rectangular, whereas animal cells are smaller and irregular in shape. Whilst both cell types have a cell membrane, plant cells also have a rigid cell wall (usually) that supports the plant as it reaches towards the sun. In contrast, animals, with their internal or external skeletons and the need to move, do not have cell walls that provide support and rigidity.

Plant and animal cells are both eukaryotic; that is, they contain membrane-bound organelles. The most important of these is the nucleus that carries the organism's genetic information. Other organelles common to both cell types include: ribosomes; endoplasmic reticulum; Golgi apparatus; and peroxisomes. Both types of cells are filled with cytoplasm, a jelly-like fluid.

Plant cells are autotrophic. They contain chloroplasts, organelles that produce simple sugars by photosynthesis. Animal cells cannot make their own food, relying on glucose molecules to be transported to the cell. **In both cases** the mitochondria break down the sugars to release energy.

Animal cells have one or more small vacuoles that store water, ions and waste, whereas plant cells usually have one large central vacuole that can take up to 90% of cell volume. In plant cells, the vacuoles store water and maintain turgidity of the cell.

describing

purpose

giving a detailed account of the properties/qualities/features/parts of something

things to know

A concept map is a useful tool for planning a description.

Descriptions are written in the present tense if they are about something that continues to exist or an ongoing situation. They use past tense if they are about something or a situation that no longer exists.

sentence starters

An examination of ... reveals ...

Upon examination, it can be seen that ...

One of the characteristics of ... is ...

... has a number of distinguishing/special/unique/notable features, including ...

The most obvious/prominent/significant feature/element of ... is ...

The key/most obvious feature(s) of ... is/are ...

... has several distinguishing features, which include ...

The major attribute of ... is ...

... has some distinctive features/characteristics that make it unique.

... comprises/is composed of/consists of/is constructed of ...

... has some very distinctive traits, especially ...

... is unlike any other ...

... looks like ...

Other important aspects are ...

Other less important/obvious features are ...

useful scientific vocabulary

additionally	described/ description	important	revealed
also	displayed	like/unlike	some/sometimes
appeared/ appearance	examined/ examination	obvious	the following characteristics
can/could	feature	occurred	unique/uniquely
combined	happened	part	visually
comprised	impact	properties	

example

A camel **has a number of unique features**. The camel's physical adaptations have evolved to cope with desert conditions. **The most obvious feature of** the camel is its hump(s) that stores fat, allowing the animal to go for days without food and water. When the camel finds water, it can rehydrate quickly. Camels are omnivorous, able to eat almost anything, no matter how salty or thorny. Sometimes called "ships of the desert", camels are capable of travelling long distances.

Desert environments can become very hot during the day. The camel's thick coat and long legs minimise heat absorption from the sun and hot ground, whilst the lack of body fat outside the hump(s) prevents the retention of heat in the body.

Many deserts are sandy, so camels have thick foot pads to prevent them from sinking into the sand. Additionally, their long eyelashes, ear hair and sealable nostrils form a barrier against the sand. The nostrils also trap water vapour from the exhaled breath for reuse in the body.

explaining

purpose

making an idea or situation clear by showing **what** it is (description), **how** it works (process) and **why** it works or occurs (reasons)

things to know

When planning an explanation, it can be helpful to sort your ideas into three categories, labelled 'what', 'how' and 'why'.

Explanations often include descriptions, procedures and a justification. The information on those pages may also be useful.

sentence starters

This process/situation/event is called ...

There are several aspects to the ..., particularly ...

The factors that contribute to this situation include ...

The main effect of ... is ...

They are most likely to occur when ...

As a result of ..., ... occurs.

The process is/starts with ...

The steps involved are ...

The (current) situation exists because ...

... works by ...

... usually occur when/if ...

There are several reasons for ...

... has multiple causes, which include ...

... is like this because ...

The main reason that ... occurs is ...

This happens/has happened because ...

The reason for this situation is ...

To put it simply, ... is/are caused by ...

If ... were to change, then ... would happen.

useful scientific vocabulary

- accounted (for)
- affect/affected
- acts/acted as/like
- as
- because
- called
- caused/causing
- consequence/consequently
- created
- detailed/details
- effect (of)
- ensured (that)
- explained/explanation
- generally
- happened
- hence
- how
- interpreted/interpretation
- if ... then ...
- lead (present tense)/led (past tense) to
- known as
- occurred
- often
- outcome
- particularly
- phenomenon/phenomena
- process
- prompted
- provided (that)
- rarely
- reason (for)
- resulted (from)/results (of)/resulting
- some/sometimes
- supported (by)
- what
- why

example

In the past 200 years, the world has been warming. **This process** of global warming **is** caused by a natural phenomenon **called** the greenhouse effect.

The Earth's climate is driven by a continuous flow of energy, including ultraviolet radiation, from the sun. During the day, the ultraviolet radiation from the sun passes through the Earth's atmosphere and warms the Earth's surface. As the surface temperature rises, the heat energy radiates back into the atmosphere. Some of this heat (as infra-red radiation) is absorbed by a naturally occurring layer of atmospheric gases such as carbon dioxide, water vapour, methane, nitrous oxide, ozone and halocarbons. This layer, often called greenhouse gases, acts as a blanket trapping the heat. It shields the Earth from the cold of the universe, particularly at night when there is no sun.

If the quantity of greenhouse gases in the atmosphere increases, then the layer gets thicker, acting like an extra blanket warming the earth. Prolonged global warming can lead to rising land temperatures causing longer droughts, more bush fires, and a spread in tropical diseases. It is also likely to cause increased ocean temperatures resulting in glaciers and polar ice caps melting, rises in sea levels, more cyclones and flooding, and changes in ocean currents. Increased temperatures will also affect the survival of plants and animals, on land and in the sea. The higher temperatures will favour some organisms and cause others to change their behaviour or die out.

falsifying

purpose

demonstrating that a general statement is incorrect by using one or more counter-examples

things to know

Experimental results and observations can be used to support or disprove hypotheses. This is the basis of experimental design (see pages 8 and 9). The better (more quantifiable or measurable) the hypothesis, the better the falsification and experimental design opportunities.

sentence starters

The results of the experiment confirmed ...

These observations do not support ...

The hypothesis needs to be modified to ...

The results limited ...

This suggests that further research/investigations is/are necessary

Whilst the results appear to negate/refute/disprove/falsify ..., further investigation is needed to ...

The experimental procedures need to be examined before concluding that ...

The conjecture/hypothesis that ...

If a single case/example of ... were found, then the conjecture would be falsified.

useful scientific vocabulary

certain/certainty	doubt	negate	tested/testable
concluded/ conclusion	false/falsification/ falsified/falsify	null/nullify	theory
conjecture	generalised/ generalisation	proved/disproved	universal
correct/incorrect	hypothesis/ hypotheses	refuted/refutation	validity
counter-example	inductive/ inductively	rejected	verify/verified/ verification

example

In 1959, Karl Popper was the first to discuss the imbalance between verifying and falsifying (synonyms for falsify are negate, disprove, refute or nullify). He used a now famous example of white swans. Popper argued that a European scientist who observed that every swan he had seen was white might have concluded that all swans are white. This is an example of inductive reasoning (see pages 36 and 37). The statement is called a universal generalisation. However, the scientist could not be certain that all swans are white because it was impractical to find every swan to verify that each of them was white.

The conjecture that all swans are white can be tested because it can be falsified. **If a single** black (or pink or green or any other colour) swan **were found, then the conjecture would be falsified** by that counter-example. Of course, before accepting the falsification, there are questions that must be answered. For instance, could the bird be a different species – if the bird is pink, it might be a flamingo. Alternatively, is the observation reliable – if the swan is green, it might be because its feathers are coated in algae.

Scientists do not discuss universal generalisations using language that indicates certainty (see the modality table on page 52), even though they may be considered to be 'beyond reasonable doubt'. For example, modern thinking about the evolution of species is described as a theory even though almost all biologists accept its validity. In the debates about the health hazards of smoking or climate change linked to human activity, scientists are reluctant to say there is certainty. Opponents have exploited this as evidence of significant doubt about the conclusions.

inferring

purpose

using what is known to make meaning or arrive at an answer, uncovering the answer even though it is not directly said or stated

things to know

Inference is the process used to reach a conclusion. It is determined by what you observe and what your previous experience or knowledge tells you. That is why two people may observe the same things but reach different conclusions.

In writing about inference, you should state what you observe (using all your senses and appropriate measuring instruments) or have read, and what background knowledge you are utilising, and then describe what you infer and why. It is reasonable to suggest alternative conclusions in case your inference is incorrect.

sentence starters

The text/results show(s) that ...

The diagram/photograph shows that ...

It can be inferred that ...

It means that ...

It is well known that ...

Several facts are relevant to this situation: ...

It is reasonable to assume that ...

The interpretation of ... is supported by ...

This interpretation is supported by the following evidence:

A trend was observed ...

The relationship between ... and ... was ...

There was a connection between ... and ...

An exception to the trend was ...

It is likely that ... because ...

There are several interpretations, including ...

... has several possible interpretations; however, ... is the most likely.

Whilst ..., it is possible to infer that ...

Without knowledge of ..., it could be inferred that ...

useful scientific vocabulary

appearance	deduced/deduction	inferred/inference	shows
assumed (that)	example	interpreted/ interpretation	since
caused	however	reason (for)	surmise
concluded (that)	identified	resulted	therefore
consequently	implied	revealed	while/whilst
could	indirect	seemed	

example

There is a **photograph that shows** a bird inside the open mouth of a crocodile *[the photograph is of an Egyptian Plover inside the open mouth of a Nile crocodile; it can be found by searching the internet]*.

It is well known that crocodiles are carnivorous. They hunt by stealth to catch their prey and then use their strong jaws to bite and tear it apart. Less well known is that the arrangement of the crocodiles' teeth and jaws does not allow them to chew their food, nor can they use their tongues to move the food around their mouths. This can result in food scraps becoming trapped in their teeth.

Symbiosis is a close and often long-term interaction between two different biological species. Mutualism is a form of symbiosis in which both species benefit. For example, dogs and humans have a mutualistic relationship where the humans provide food and shelter and the dogs provide protection, companionship and assistance with some tasks.

Whilst the photograph does not show what happens next, **it is possible to infer that** the photograph shows an example of a symbiotic relationship between the bird and the crocodile. If crocodiles have food stuck in their teeth, they can suffer from tooth decay and possible infection and pain. When the crocodile sits motionlessly on the river bank with an open mouth, the Egyptian Plover flies into the mouth to eat the food scraps caught in the teeth of the crocodile.

Without knowledge of symbiosis **it could be inferred that** the crocodile might attempt to eat any bird that came within its reach. This symbiotic relationship is therefore remarkable because the crocodile does not attempt to eat the bird, which flies away unharmed.

justifying

purpose

showing or proving that a decision, action or idea about something is reasonable or necessary by giving sound, logical and appropriate reasons for it

things to know

A complete justification describes the decision and then provides the reasons for that decision. It answers the question 'why?'.

It explains why you support a course of action or have a particular belief. Your justification may be the result of inductive or deductive thinking.

sentence starters

There are several/many reasons for ...

The weight of evidence would suggest that ...

Consequently, it would seem better to ... because ...

... is a valid recommendation/suggestion based on ...

... is a better option because ...

The reasons that support the choice of ... are based on factual evidence.

... is a good idea because ...

The best decision is ... because ...

... is a reasonable course of action because ...

... shows an intelligent response to the problem/issue/topic of ...

Circumstances suggest the following course of action because ...

... is well supported by the evidence, which states that ...

For now, ... is the better option because ...

useful scientific vocabulary

acted/action	deduced/deduction	logic/logical/ logically	substantiated
assumed	demonstrated/ demonstration	plausible	supported
calculated/ calculations	disproved by	produces	using
confirmed/confirms	explain why	proposition	validated
correct	find	proof/proved	verified
counter-example	justified/justification	reasons/reasonable/ reasoning	why
decision	likely	similarly	

example

The rusting wrecks of ships sunk during World War II create a high risk of serious environmental damage. Action to prevent leakages of dangerous substances carried by the ships must be urgently investigated. **There are several reasons for** this decision.

During World War II 1554 ships were sunk*. All of these vessels contained fuel, and many carried explosives and toxic cargoes. They have now been in a corrosive environment for more than 70 years. It is likely that corrosion will release these dangerous and polluting substances into the marine environment.

The cost of environmental damage through uncontrolled leakage of these dangerous substances and pollutants will be high. It is likely to outweigh the cost of locating the wrecks and either sealing them to prevent leakages or removing the dangerous substances*.

Action is needed at both an international and a local level. Given the global nature of the problem, the United Nations should be the body to coordinate the action.

**Citation(s) providing the source(s) of this information or evidence for these assertion(s) would normally be included here.*

[Note that this example uses the same content as the example of arguing on pages 22 and 23. Compare the two and note the similarities and differences in language use because of the different purposes for writing.]

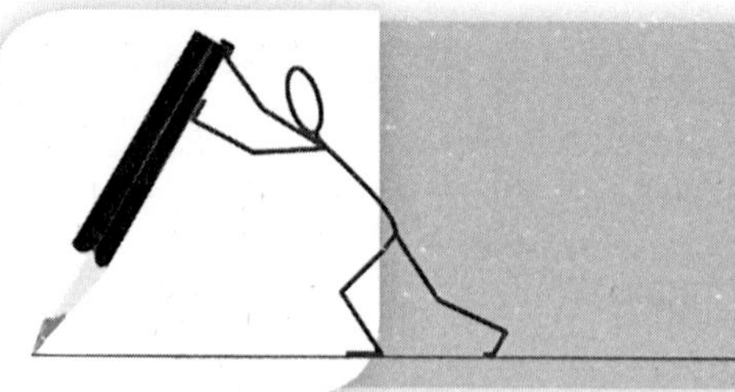

reasoning inductively

purpose

using a small number of observations to identify a logical pattern and infer a larger theory

things to know

Inductive reasoning is the scientific companion of deductive reasoning (pages 16 and 17) and falsification (pages 30 and 31). It differs from deductive reasoning mainly because the conclusions can be false even though all the premises (evidence, facts or assumptions) are true. The outcome of inductive reasoning is that the conclusions are either strong or weak, not true or false.

Inductive reasoning is limited because we do not observe the universe at all times and in all places. It cannot lead to proof because we are not justified in making a general rule from the observation of particular cases. The conclusions of inductive reasoning are described using probability – how likely it is that they are true (refer to modality table on page 52).

sentence starters

The evidence/observations show/shows that ...

It is suggested that ...

This coincided with ...

... is linked to ...

... increased/decreased the likelihood of ...

... fits this pattern.

... may have been caused by ...

It can be concluded that ...

If ... then ...

On the basis of this evidence, it is predicted/concluded that ...

One theory is that ...

Some questions are unanswered by this theory: ...

useful scientific vocabulary

argued/argument	falsified/falsification	otherwise	resulted (in)/results (of)
accepted	for example	particular	simultaneously
assumed/assumption	for instance	pattern	suggested
caused by	generally	predicted	supported
concluded/conclusion	induced/induction	premise	typically
conjecture	likelihood	probability	theory
due to	modified/modification	proposition	therefore
evidence	observed/observation	rejected/rejection	
fact	occurred	required/requirement	

example

The observations: Fossil **evidence shows that** at the end of the Cretaceous period many organisms, including the dinosaurs, became extinct. **This coincided with** a global climate change from a warm, mild climate to a cooler, variable one. Geological **observations show that,** in many places around the world, the rocks formed at the end of the Cretaceous period contain a thin layer of clay with an unusually high iridium content. **It is suggested that** this clay **may have been caused by** a massive terrestrial disturbance. The disturbance threw rocks, dust, soot and toxic gases into the air, which obscured the sun and caused acid rain. This is likely to have led to the global climate change noted earlier, causing the extinction of any plants and animals unable to adapt to the new weather patterns.

The pattern: Additional geological evidence from the end of the Cretaceous period **fits this pattern**. Shocked quartz has been found in some rocks, possibly caused by pressure waves so powerful that they rearranged the crystal structure of the rocks. Other rocks contain glassy spheres that look like molten rock that solidified into droplets when it cooled. Finally, a soot layer has been found in many areas, suggesting widespread fires.

The asteroid theory: **One theory is that** a series of asteroids and meteors, some very large, collided with the Earth, their impact throwing up enough dust to cause global climate change. Asteroids are higher in iridium content than the Earth's crust, so the iridium layer could have been formed from the dust of a vaporised asteroid. A crater has been found in the Gulf of Mexico of sufficient size to have had global impact.

Possible falsification: **Some questions are unanswered by this theory**. Why did some organisms survive the mass extinction whilst others died out? Is there evidence of bombardment of the earth by meteors at the relevant time? Can we be certain about the timing and sequence of the events, given the lack of precision in dating rocks? Are there other explanations for the evidence (there are other theories)? The answers to any of these questions could result in falsification of the asteroid theory, leading to its modification or rejection.

writing more complex documents

Cohesive scientific writing involves the skills of writing individual sections in a variety of styles and combining them into a sophisticated and meaningful product. Most scientific writing fits one of four types.

Experimental reports may include an introduction, aim, research, hypotheses, experimental design, method, results, discussion, recommendations, and conclusions – the combination of the ten forms of writing described on pages 2 to 21. In fact, the ten examples of writing on those pages, when combined with some linking sentences (see pages 39 and 40) and a reference list, make up an experimental report.

Large-scale investigations start by introducing the topic and examining the relevant research. They usually include a series of experiments, followed by an evaluation of the results and conclusions.

Research involves using secondary data and considering the scholarly ideas and work of others to induce or deduce findings.

Persuasive or argumentative essays pose a question or problem then draw on theory, observations and deductive reasoning to either canvass the arguments for and against an issue or to argue in favour of a preferred solution.

Abstracts are usually required in a lengthy document. The abstract is the last part of the writing process. To write an abstract, summarise the information in each section in one or two short sentences. Then read the abstract to ensure that it covers the important points in the document. Check the word length prescribed for the abstract (this can vary, but is usually from 100 to 250 words) and further reduce the number of words, if needed, by removing unnecessary words or rewriting some of the sentences into a single, more succinct sentence. Check that the abstract does not contain any unexplained abbreviations. Finally, edit the abstract to ensure that it flows and is not repetitive in content or vocabulary.

linking the sections of a large document

explanation

Lengthy documents have many sections. Each section should have a heading, and sub-headings may also be used. A table of contents listing the sections is essential.

A lengthy document is easier to navigate if there are links between sections reminding the reader of what has gone before and foreshadowing what is coming next. This is called *signposting*, and can be particularly helpful for the reader if they are interrupted while reading the document, or if they choose to read some sections out of order (many teachers read the first and last sections first, and then go back to look at the detail in the middle of the document).

examples of signposting

The introductory section should end with a paragraph describing what is to come in the rest of the document. The information on writing introductions (pages 2 and 3) may assist in writing this paragraph. An example of such a signposting paragraph is:

> This experimental report contains five sections. Following this introduction, some background research is presented, leading to the development of six hypotheses about the rusting of steel. The second section on experimental process describes the experimental design, procedures and method, followed by a third section that presents the observed data. In the discussion section, the data are analysed and deductions are made. The report ends with recommendations to prevent the corrosion of steel and a conclusion.

Additionally, each section needs an opening sentence that links it to the preceding section, for example:

> The previous section presented the data collected in the experiment. This section analyses and discusses these data.

At the end of each section, the final paragraph should provide a link to the next section, for example:

> This section having described the procedure used to conduct the experiment, the next section presents the results of that experiment.

Finally, the last paragraph in the concluding section should summarise the entire document, for example:

> This paper has detailed an experiment that investigated the effect of atmospheric and other conditions on rusting. The introductory section explained the topic, discussed rusting in the wider context of corrosion, and defined some other key terms. The aim of this experiment was two-fold: (a) to determine the conditions that promote the corrosion of steel; and (b) to find how corrosion can be prevented or reduced. In Section 2, six hypotheses were proposed to give effect to these aims. The third section reported on the design and method of several experiments examining the effect on rusting of water, air and salt and testing some options for preventing or minimising corrosion of steel. The results of these experiments were presented in Section 4. The discussion in Section 5 showed that the hypotheses were all confirmed. To summarise, exposure to water and air was necessary for steel to corrode. The following conditions increased the rate of corrosion: exposure to salt; larger surface area; deformation of the steel; and contact with a less reactive metal. Corrosion can be prevented or reduced by: thorough removal of salt after contact; coating of the steel surface to prevent contact with water and air; and the use of a 'sacrificial' more reactive metal. The penultimate section contained recommendations on how rusting can be prevented or minimised.

Signposting sentences use past tense for earlier sections and present tense for the sections yet to come. Allow for signposting sentences and paragraphs in any word limit for the document.

planning scientific writing

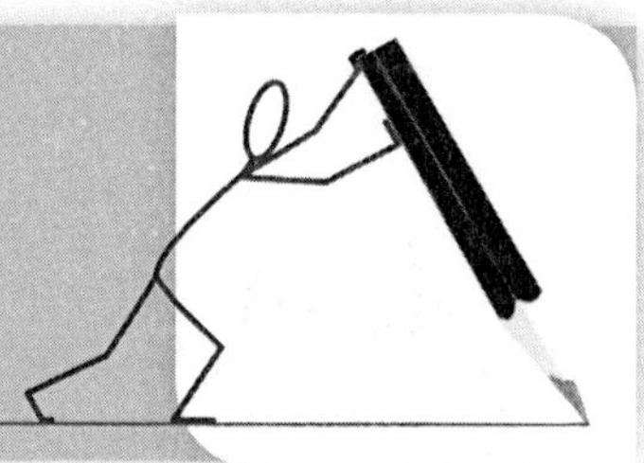

knowledge of the topic.

If you know nothing about a topic, you cannot write about it. So the first step in preparing a scientific document is to research (find out about) the topic. Depending on your teacher's instructions you may do this by yourself or in a group. Some background reading is essential. Do not start your research at a complex level – often your teacher's advice or a textbook is a good place to begin.

Some questions that can be used when planning your writing include:

- What do I know?
- What do the important words mean (including the task words)?
- What are the problems associated with this issue?
- Why is it important?
- What factors seem to have an influence?
- How can I find out more?

A concept map is a good way to summarise your knowledge of a topic. If you are working in a group, you need to find out the total knowledge of the group. A brainstorming exercise can be useful, making sure that everyone has a chance to contribute. Another strategy is to ask everyone to prepare their own concept map and then combine them. It can be useful to show your teacher the completed concept map and ask questions such as, 'Do you think I have enough information?' and 'Have I missed out anything important?'.

Wikipedia is often frowned upon as a research source, but it can be a useful introduction to the important issues. However, it should not be the only source of information. Many regard Wikipedia as lacking credibility. Further, much of the information is written at a readability level that is too high for most school students. It can be tempting to copy information when it is too difficult to process. Simple English Wikipedia contains information written at an easier level.

If you are researching on the internet, you need to evaluate the quality of information found at the various websites. If you do not know how to do this, ask your school librarian or your teacher for advice.

purpose of the writing

Once you know something about the topic, you should consider the type of document you will be writing – in other words, what is your purpose for writing? Your teacher's instructions (either in class or in the written description of the assessment task) will be important here. There are many purposes of writing, for example, presenting an argument for a course of action, solving a problem, or investigating an issue. Consider what sections are needed in the document and then use the preceding pages in this book to help you plan and write each section.

audience

You also need to decide on your audience. In many forms of scientific writing at school the audience is your teacher, fellow students, or some other person with a reasonable knowledge of the topic. This means that you can use most scientific words without having to explain what they mean. However, in some cases you might be asked to write for younger students or the general public (who cannot be assumed to know anything about science). Knowing your audience will affect the level of explanation and detail you provide and the language you use.

action

Plan how you will complete the document by the due date. If working in a group, decide who will write which section and the date by which it will be completed. Think about the order in which the different parts must be written. Introductions, conclusions and abstracts are usually written last. Allow time for proofreading, corrections and printing, and agree on who will do this. If working by yourself, set a timetable so that you can do a little each day rather than a last minute rushed job.

writing to a word limit

Most assessment tasks have a word limit, for three reasons:

- It indicates the extent of the detail expected. Longer tasks suggest that points should be developed in more detail, not necessarily that there should be more points.

- The teacher marking the work that you and other students have submitted does not have the time needed to read excessively long documents.
- Writing to length is an important skill to learn, in science and elsewhere. It shows that you can use your judgement to select the important information.

If your document is too long your grade may be reduced. The marker may stop reading after the required word length has been reached, so you will not receive credit for information provided at the end of the document. Finally, scientific writing should be concise, so you may be penalised for sentence structures that use more words than necessary. On the other hand, if your document is too short, it is likely that it will not contain enough information, again reducing the grade you receive.

An A4 page typed using standard fonts and spacings contains approximately 500 words. There is usually a 10% tolerance in word limits. That means if the limit is stated as 1000 words, then 1100 words will usually be accepted. Word counts do not usually include any text in the abstract, appendices, attachments, footnotes, endnotes or reference lists (although the word count produced by a word processor will include them). However, you should check this with your teacher.

When planning your writing, you should also plan how many words you will write in each section in order to meet your target word count. The following guidelines may be useful.

- The introduction should take about 10% of the word limit.
- The number of words devoted to each point will vary according to the amount of information available and the level of detail expected. A reasonable guide for shorter tasks (those with a word count of 2000 words or less) is 150–200 words. However, longer word limits indicate that points should be developed in more detail (and hence more words), not necessarily that there should be more points.
- Remember to allow space for signposting sentences and paragraphs (see pages 39 and 40).
- The conclusion should take about 10% to 15% of the word limit.

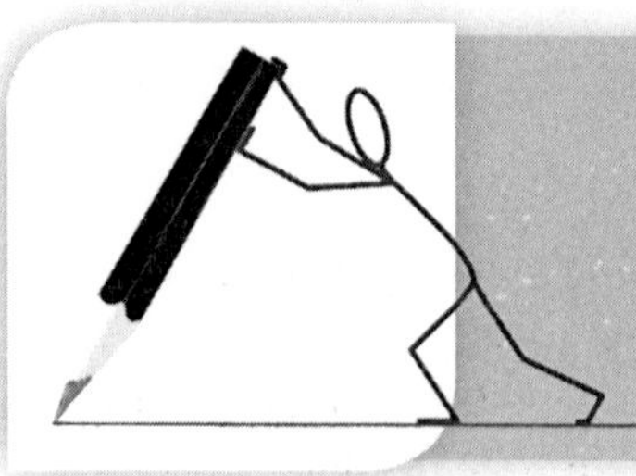

scientific data

scientific observation

Scientific observation is the process of collecting information (data). It involves receiving information through any of the five senses: sight, sound, touch, smell, and taste (taking appropriate safety precautions). Scientific instruments such as microscopes, telescopes, cameras, or radiation sensors may be used to extend the range of phenomena that can be observed. Observations can be quantified by counting or by measurement, using instruments such as tape measures, measuring cylinders, thermometers, scales, and light, sound and/or electrical meters.

Scientific information may be quantitative or qualitative. Quantitative data are recorded as numbers, obtained by counting (called frequency) and measuring. Qualitative data are recorded in words and are descriptive, for example, appearance, texture, smell, and taste, or may record the absence or presence of a property. Provided that appropriate experimental procedures are used, quantitative data are objective, that is, they do not require the use of judgement by the person collecting the data. However, qualitative data require interpretation by the person collecting the data (for example, would everyone describe a particular odour or flavour the same way?). Consequently, qualitative data may be less reliable than quantitative data.

Scientific information may also be classified as primary or secondary. Primary data are collected specifically for a particular experiment or study, usually by the person or team undertaking the research. Secondary data are usually collected by someone else and is not solely for the use of a particular experiment or study. For example, the information publicly available from the Australian Bureau of Statistics (population and economic data), the Bureau of Meteorology (climate data), or Geoscience Australia (geological data) are all examples of secondary data.

visual data displays

Data, when first collected, are usually in raw (unsorted) form, making them hard to interpret. To make meaning of the data, we usually need to transform them into visual displays such as tables, graphs, maps, and diagrams. Visual data displays are also helpful in supporting explanations – it is true that a picture is worth a thousand words. As it is beyond the scope of this book to explain how to prepare these visual displays, this book is limited to how to seamlessly weave data displays into written scientific texts.

There are conventions for the use of diagrams in science. Unnecessary detail is removed to focus attention on what matters; for example, a diagram of chemical apparatus is simplified by presenting it in only two dimensions.

All visual displays need titles and labels. Titles explain what the visual display is about, and may include when or where the data were collected. Labels give more detailed information. In tables, the labels are usually row and column headings. In graphs, labels are used to explain the interpretation of the axes and/or the scale. In maps and some graphs, labels are used to explain the meaning of symbols and shading (called a legend or key). Labels (annotations) may also be used to identify parts of the display that are of particular interest, especially in diagrams.

Visual data displays should be large enough for the detail to be read easily. One third of a page is suitable for most purposes, but some tables or diagrams may need to be larger. The data display should be located in between paragraphs, close to the relevant text. Where possible, keep a table on one page and do not allow a row to straddle two pages. Visual data displays are usually numbered, for example Figure 1, or Table 3.2. Lengthy documents may include a list of tables and figures near the table of contents.

The text of the document should refer to the data display, otherwise why was it included? Sentence starters that can be used to link the text to a data display include:

> Table/Figure ‹*number*› shows that ...
>
> As can be seen from Table/Figure ‹*number*› ...
>
> ..., shown in Table/Figure ‹*number*›, ...
>
> The information has/data have been tabulated/graphed in Table/Figure ‹*number*›.
>
> Table/Figure ‹*number*› shows a clear trend ...
>
> Table/Figure ‹*number*› shows a strong connection/relationship between ...
>
> Figure ‹*number*› illustrates how ...

These sentence starters can be adapted by using the substitutes for 'showed that' found on page 51.

If presenting secondary data, or reproducing a diagram found in another document, it is essential to show the source immediately underneath the table or visual display and to include it in the list of references.

plagiarism, citations and references

plagiarism

Plagiarism is a serious and reprehensible activity. It occurs when sections of text are copied, and imported into one's own work with limited or no acknowledgement of the origin of the information. Even if ideas have been reworked into your own language, they are still not your original ideas, so attempting to pass them off as yours is regarded as plagiarism. If you copy anything more than a phrase (approximately ten words) without using direct quotes you are copying, not only someone else's ideas, but the unique way that they express them.

To avoid plagiarism, ensure that everything you write is in your own words. If you copy a diagram from the internet, acknowledge the source. Keep notes of all the sources of information you consulted during your research so that you can list them in the references section at the end of the document.

Some websites contain very complicated information. If you do not understand what you are reading, do not be tempted to cut and paste the text into your document. Your teacher will know what you are capable of understanding and will recognise when you have not written it yourself. Look for a simpler source of information.

Given this advice, you might ask how much of the sentence starters and useful words in this book can be used in your writing? They can be copied because they provide *ways of saying* something. The words and phrases are not unique to a particular writer and do not use the ideas of someone else. They are acceptable because of their generic nature. As you develop your skills and confidence as a scientific writer, you will rely less and less on the reusable language in this book.

citations and references

References give the source of quotations and other information used in a document and are listed in detail in a separate section at the end of the document. They are an important way of providing evidence. A citation is a code embedded in the text of the document, usually in brackets, for example (Smith, 2014) or [23]. It links to a source listed in the reference section. In the case of a direct quote from a source, the citation also includes the page number(s) where the original text can be found.

All references should provide: author(s) name(s); date of publication; title; and publication details. There are many different ways or styles of formatting citations and references: Harvard and CSE (Council of Science Editors) are commonly used in the sciences; Chicago is commonly used in the arts and humanities; and APA (American Psychological Association) is commonly used in psychology and the social sciences, including education. Your teacher or school librarian can explain your school's preferred citation style.

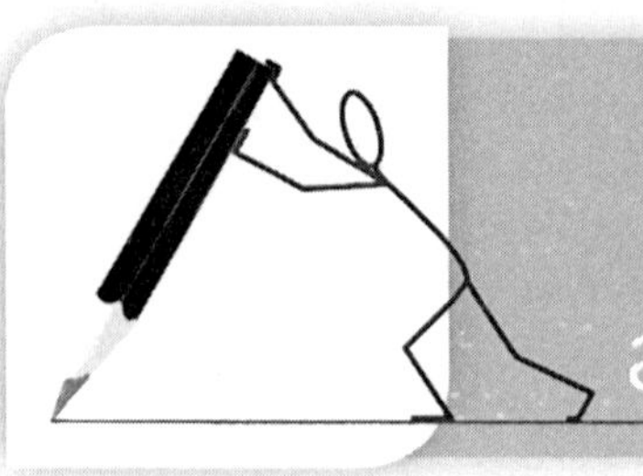

examples of what to avoid in scientific writing

imprecise words: a bit; a few; a little; a lot; about; around; heaps; highly; loads; lots; many; masses; moment; roughly; several; some

overused words: absolutely (unless part of a technical term); actually; amazing; awesome; fine; good/bad; got; interesting; like; literally; major; nice; quite; really; said; very; well

foreign words and phrases: inter alia; prima facie; faux pas; fait accompli; a priori

personal pronouns: I; me; you; she; her; he; him; it; we; us; you; they; them; myself; yourself; himself; herself; itself; ourselves; yourselves; themselves; my; his; her; its; mine; hers; our; your; their; ours; yours; theirs

contractions: aren't; can't; couldn't; didn't; doesn't; don't; hadn't; hasn't; haven't; he'd; he'll; he's; I'd; I'll; I'm; I've; isn't; it's; let's; mightn't; mustn't; shan't; she'd; she'll; she's; shouldn't; that's; there's; they'd; they'll; they're; they've; we'd; we're; we've; weren't; what'll; what're; what's; what've; where's; who's; who'll' who're; who's; who've; won't; wouldn't; you'd; you'll; you're; you've

double negatives: I can't get no satisfaction

prolixity (unnecessary words): actually; after due consideration; as a matter of fact; as far as ... is concerned; basically; basis; on the basis that; by and large; cannot help but; in (under) the circumstances; comparatively; currently, presently; cut back; doubtless, undoubtedly; due to; effectively; (due to) the fact that; goes without saying; in the final analysis; hitherto; if and when; literally; marginally; may well be; needless to say; not necessarily; obviously; overly; period of; personally; in point of fact; point (moment) in time; in the process of; put an end to; the reason is because; reason why; relatively; in spite of; ten in number; there is no alternative but; to all intents and purposes; to the tune of; utilise; very; as to whether; well and truly; whether or not

examples of what to avoid in scientific writing

clichés: a far cry from; abject failure; acid test; across the board; ample opportunity; as a matter of fact; back to basics; back to the drawing board; ballpark figure; be all and end all; benefit of the doubt; big picture; bottom line; by and large; by the book; cut both ways; cutting edge; despite my best efforts; dos and don'ts; easier said than done; ground breaking; high hopes; ins and outs; last but not least; law of averages; lion's share; moment of truth; part and parcel; proof of the pudding; proving ground; reinvent the wheel; saving grace; stumbling block; take pains; test of time; the exception proves the rule; the root of the matter; tip of the iceberg; to and fro; too numerous to mention; tried and tested; user-friendly; wait and see; winning streak

tautologies (words that mean the same thing): absolutely essential; added bonus; advance planning; advance warning; all-time record; ask the question; bits and pieces; blend together; brief moment; cancel out; circle around; close proximity; combine together; could possibly; drop down; each and every; estimated at about; final outcome; first and foremost; first priority; full to capacity; gather together; join together; lag behind; lift up; like ilk; might possibly; minute detail; necessary requirement; never before; new innovation; none at all; past experience; period of time; plan ahead; present time; puzzling problem; raise up; reiterate again; revert back; short summary; small in size; still persists; 6.00 am in the morning; 6.00 pm in the afternoon; sum total; the vast majority; true facts; twelve noon/midnight; ultimate goal

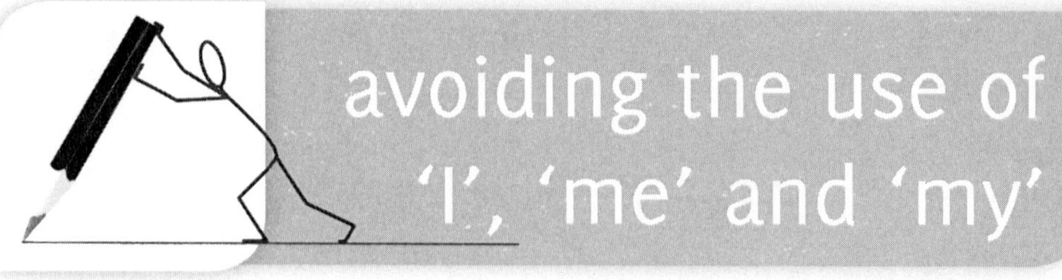

avoiding the use of 'I', 'me' and 'my'

explanation

In most forms of formal, scientific writing, the use of the **first person** (I, me or my) is generally discouraged. More authority is given to the work if it is written in the **third person.** In addition, the use of the **passive voice** (i.e., the 'doer' is removed) is also a prominent feature of scientific texts. The phrases below provide some ways to avoid the use of the first person.

ways of saying

It could be suggested that ...

This is/can be illustrated by ...

It is seen through ...

This is evident when ...

Upon examination, it becomes apparent that ...

The facts indicate that ...

This is exemplified by ...

This illustrates that ...

This shows that ...

Therefore, it can be stated that ...

This becomes apparent when ...

With some exceptions, sources generally agree that ...

... clearly points out that ...

This is most obvious when ...

It can, therefore, be observed that ...

There is evidence to support both opinions on this topic.

Author 1 (date) agrees/disagrees with author 2 (date) that/about ...

Notable exceptions to this rule are ...

Observations reveal that ...

substitutes for 'showed that'

explanation

It is common practice in scientific writing to refer to sources of information such as data, diagrams, tables, graphs, and research by others. Relying on phrases such as, 'the graph showed that ...', 'the table showed that ...', 'the information showed that ... ', can be tedious and unsophisticated. The list below provides some alternatives.

Tense should be adjusted according the the context. Use present tense (show/s) when referring to visual displays, for example. If referring to research by others, use past tense (showed).

ways of saying

according to

affirmed that

as could be seen in ...,

claimed that

confirmed that

considered that

demonstrated that

depicted the

determined to be

displayed that

established that

exemplified the

exhibited the

explained that

exposed the

found that

gave the result that

illustrated the idea that

implied that

indicated that

it could be seen in ... that

led to the conclusion that

manifested the

presented the

proved that

provided evidence of

recorded the

reflected the

represented the

resulted in

revealed that

suggested that

validated the result that

was an example of

was consistent with

degrees of intensity (modality)

MODE	LOW →						→ HIGH
probability	impossible/ impossibly	improbable/ improbably	unlikely	possible/ possibly	likely/in all likelihood	probable/ probably	sure/surely	certain/ certainly
frequency	never	seldom	occasional/ occasionally	sometimes	often	usual/usually	regularly/in most cases	always
certainty	never	scarce/ scarcely	perhaps/in some cases	might/could	as likely as not	inevitable/ inevitably	undoubted/ undoubtedly	definite/ definitely
extent	never	scarce/ scarcely	limited	partly	general/ generally	mainly	almost	complete/ completely
confidence	suspect	unreasonable/ unreasonably	doubtful/ doubtfully	moderate/ moderately	reasonable/ reasonably	plausible/ plausibly	undeniable/ undeniably	irrefutable/ irrefutably
importance	desirable/ desirably	preferable/ preferably	required	necessary	important/ importantly	unquestionable/ unquestionably	essential/ essentially	vital/vitally
intensity	scarce/ scarcely	slight/slightly	mild/mildly	intermittent/ intermittently	moderate/ moderately	typical/ typically	unrelenting/ unrelentingly	extreme/ extremely

Caution: *The adjectives and adverbs in this table are often used to convey an opinion. If they are used in scientific writing, the choice of word would usually be supported by evidence.*

teacher reference: the nature of scientific writing

Scientific writing is the prose that accompanies or supports scientific arguments, experiments and investigations. Science teachers must explicitly teach this style of writing and not assume that students have learnt it elsewhere, or that it is transferable from other contexts.

Scientific writing requires conciseness, achieved by ensuring that every word 'adds value' (see examples to avoid on pages 48 and 49). The appropriate use of scientific terms, symbols, standard scientific abbreviations, tables and visual images allows the writer to convey information while keeping word usage to a minimum. The use of short sentences, headings and sub-headings also adds to conciseness and clarity.

readability of scientific texts

Reading scientific texts can be challenging for many students. This is because the reading level of a scientific text is usually higher that other types of texts. There are two main reasons for this. First, readability is influenced by sentence length. Scientific writing often needs to use strings of words to convey a single idea (for example, 'the steel nails wrapped in copper wire', or 'the extension of the spring'), which contribute to longer sentences. Further, writing in passive voice and the third person usually increases the length of a sentence. Second, readability is influenced by the number of syllables in a word. The scientific vocabulary uses polysyllabic words more frequently than everyday English (e.g. photosynthesis, seismological, acceleration, equilibrium), thus increasing reading levels.

Reading levels in scientific texts, as measured by standard indexes of readability (such as the Flesch-Kincaid Index used in Microsoft Word), can sometimes appear to be high, even if the text is not complex. One reason for this is that the reading level is increased by the inclusion of symbols. For example, the readability, as assessed by the Flesch-Kincaid Index, of a passage of 230 words including eight numbers written as symbols was reduced by a whole grade level simply by removing the numbers. Secondly, writing in point form can result in what appears to be long sentences, although broken up into several points. While the use of point form makes the text easier to understand, it increases the measured reading level. Standard readability indexes were not designed for use in scientific texts and, in consequence, are not necessarily a reliable indicator of reading complexity.

a note about the corrosion experiment

In many sections of this book the examples relate to a hypothetical corrosion experiment. The experiment was designed to provide opportunities to use particular forms of language and has been limited to fit in the available space on each page. It is not intended to be an exemplar of good pedagogical or experimental practice. Should you wish students to investigate corrosion experimentally, the authors recommend modifying the experiment to make it more comprehensive.

key task word glossary

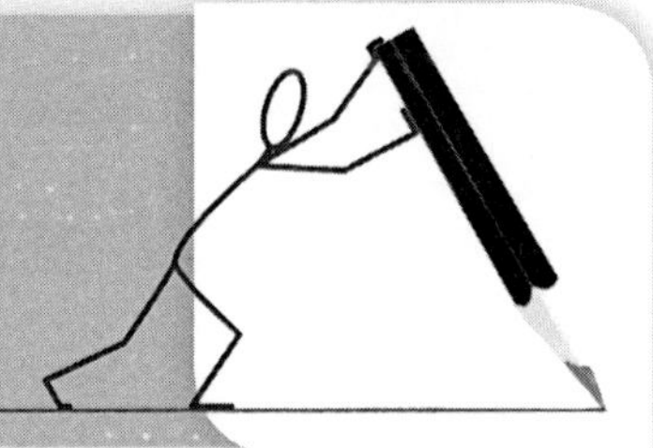

Many of these key task words give writers their purposes for writing. To fulfil each purpose successfully, students need to understand the meanings of each of these task words.

abstract	to create a general idea about something rather than one relating to a particular object, person or situation
account for	to give reasons for something and report on those reasons
account for (maths)	to report on; to try every possibility
analyse	to examine the parts of something in detail and discuss or interpret the relationship of the parts to each other and to the whole; may involve description, comparison, explanation, interpretation and critical comment
analyse (maths)	to use statistical methods to summarise, compare or infer something
appraise	to consider something or someone carefully and form an opinion about them
argue	to present one or both sides of an argument or case to reach a conclusion; may involve the use of persuasive techniques (these are factual and logical rather than emotive) to convince others that your opinion about something is the correct one
arrange	to place things into a particular position, often with a degree of order or precision
assess	to make a judgement about something based on its value or worth (may include quality, outcomes, results or size)
assume	to accept that something is true without necessarily confirming it or checking its validity
calculate	to ascertain or determine something from facts, figures or information
calculate (maths)	to obtain a result from given facts, data or other numeric information about something

categorise	to divide things or people into sets or say to which set they belong based on common criteria
classify	to group things with similarities in the same classes or categories; to defend the inclusion of similar things into these categories
comment on	to present your opinion about something
compare	to identify the ways in which two or more things are similar and different
conclude	to draw together the main ideas of something and restate them in a succinct way, often as a decision
consider	to give opinions in relation to the information you have been given about something or someone
consider (maths)	to ensure that your response refers to the particular information you have been given about something
construct	to make, build or put together items or arguments about something
contrast	to examine two or more things and focus on the differences
criticise	to make judgements about something or someone, giving details to support your views
decide	to choose something or someone based on a consideration of other possibilities
debate	to examine both sides of an issue about something and come to a conclusion – or leave the reader/listener the opportunity to come to a conclusion
deduce	to reach a conclusion about something based on evidence that is known to be true
defend	to argue in support of something
define	to show, describe or state clearly what something is and what its limits are
define (maths)	to give the meaning or precise description of the concept
demonstrate	to show something by example
describe	to give a detailed account of the properties, qualities, features or parts of something or someone
devise	to have an idea for something and design and plan it

key task word glossary

differentiate	to recognise or show the differences between one thing or person and another
differentiate (maths)	to find a derivative
discriminate	to recognise that two things or people are different
distinguish	to draw attention to, and make note of, the distinct differences between things or people
discuss	to consider the results of research and the implications of those results; to consider both sides of an issue about something, without necessarily coming to a conclusion
elaborate	to give more information or detail about something often by defining terms, giving examples and including evidence
evaluate	to consider something or someone to make a judgement of value or worth; often supported by evidence
evaluate (maths)	to find the exact value of something
examine	to look at something carefully, often for reasons 'how' or 'why' something may have happened
exemplify	to give more information or details about something
explain	to make an idea or situation clear by showing what it is (description), how it works (process) and why it works or occurs (reasons)
expound	to present a clear and convincing argument for a definite and detailed opinion about something
extend	to include or affect other people or things
extract	to obtain information from a larger amount or source of information
extrapolate	to use known facts about something as a basis for general statements about a situation or what is likely to happen in the future
extrapolate (maths)	to extend a graph to obtain additional values
generalise	to develop a broad statement that seems to be true in most situations or for most people; this does not include details such as data, quotations, or examples

generalise (maths)	to use particular examples of something to develop an equation or mathematical model to describe the overall situation
identify	to notice or discover the existence or presence of something or someone
illustrate	to use examples of something to give more detail to information or more weight to an argument
indicate	to point out something from available information
infer	to use what is known to make meaning or arrive at an answer; to uncover the answer even though it is not directly said or stated
interpret	to examine a piece of text and explain its meaning or significance, often from a particular point of view
introduce	to begin a text by describing what it is about
investigate	to examine the reasons for something
justify	to show or prove that a decision, action or idea about something is reasonable or necessary by giving sound, logical and appropriate reasons for it; answers the question 'why'
justify (maths)	to give all the logical reasons and/or mathematical arguments that have led to a decision
list	to arrange related items in order, usually under one another (i.e. vertically)
order	to arrange things in a logical way
outline	to give all the main ideas about something without the details
paraphrase	to restate what someone has said or written in a slightly different way from the way it was first stated; the meaning is retained
predict	to suggest what might happen based on the available information
prepare	to gather what you need to make ready for something that is going to happen
present	to put forward something for consideration
propose	to put forward something (e.g. a plan, an idea, a point of view, an argument, a suggestion)
prove	to support something with facts and figures

key task word glossary

prove (maths)	to produce a logical mathematical argument that shows the truth of a statement for all values or situations
quote	to repeat the exact words of the author (direct quotations) as evidence in writing
recommend	to suggest a course of action for consideration by others, providing reasons (usually the findings or research investigation) in favour of the suggestion
refer	to use material in your answer without necessarily directly quoting from the stimulus material or information
reflect	to respond in a personal way to experiences, situations, events or new information by making personal connections with the new material
sequence	to put things in the order in which things are arranged, actions are carried out, or events happen
sketch	to give the main ideas briefly about something or to create a sketch or drawing that shows the essential features; detail or accuracy is not required
solve	to find an answer or solution to a problem
suggest	to put forward or propose an idea or plan about something for someone to think about
support	to use a fact to support a statement or theory about something
summarise	to briefly state the main points in a short account with details omitted
synthesise	to put together various elements (from several places or sources) to make a whole; the reassembled material is original
trace	to show how events/arguments progress and develop
value	to establish the worth of something or someone
verify	to back up a particular result and prove something
verify (maths)	to test the truth of something

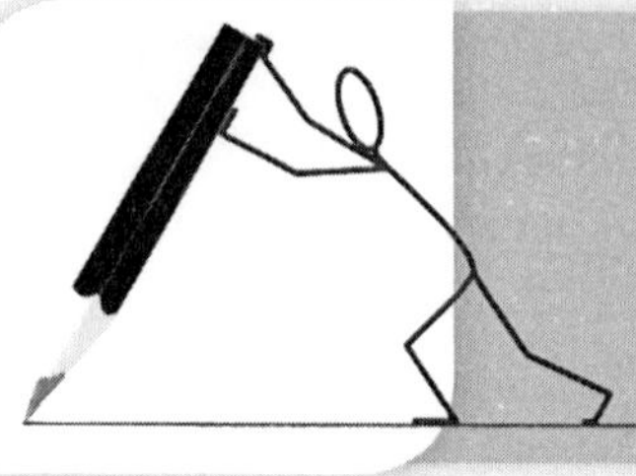

scientific glossary

abstract	1. Involving general ideas or qualities rather than specific objects or processes. 2. A summary of the contents of a book, article, or report.
accurate	The accuracy of a *measurement* is its closeness to the true value. The accuracy of an *experiment* depends on the validity of the experimental procedure and the sensitivity of the instruments used. Results are accurate if a) appropriate measuring instruments are used, b) measurements are close to the true value and c) the results can be substantiated in valid secondary sources.
bibliography	A list of sources, such as books, articles, and websites, consulted in the process of preparing a document. The difference between a bibliography and a reference list is that the bibliography may contain sources that are not cited in the document. They were used in the pre-internet days to direct the reader to possible areas of further reading, but are less common now that internet-based searches are available.
citation	An alphanumeric code embedded in the text of a scholarly document, usually in brackets. A citation links to a source document listed in the reference section. As there are several ways of formatting citations, students should check with their teacher about the preferred citation format (style).
concise	Providing information clearly, but with a minimum of words.
conclusion	1. A fact determined by a cause and effect or reasoning process. In an 'if ... then ... ' statement, the conclusion is what follows 'then'. 2. The last paragraph(s) of a document that summarises and ends the discussion.

scientific glossary

datum (singular)/data (plural)	a fact/statistic (datum) or facts/statistics (data) collected for reference or analysis. Datum is singular and rarely used. Data can be used a a singular term (eg data is ...) or a plural term (eg data are ...) and both are well accepted. To use the word as a plural, think of it as a term representing items.
empirical	Empirical evidence is information acquired by observation or experimentation.
experiment	An organised series of steps (procedure) conducted under controlled conditions to test (verify or refute) the validity of a hypothesis. Experiments rely on repeatable procedures and logical analyses of the results.
fact	A scientific fact is a phenomenon that can be observed and measured.
formal language	Formal language is used when writing for serious, professional or academic purposes. It involves the precise use of vocabulary and grammar and an impersonal, polite tone. For example, formal language does not use colloquialisms or contractions and tends to minimise the use of first person pronouns such as 'I' or 'we'.
hypothesis	A scientific hypothesis is an 'educated guess', based on prior knowledge and observation, to explain a natural phenomenon. It is the initial building block of scientific method. A scientific hypothesis must be capable of being verified or falsified by observation or experimentation. The plural of hypothesis is hypotheses.
law	A description of an observed phenomenon that holds true every time it is tested, for example, the law of gravity. A law describes what is observed, not how or why it occurs.
observation	The process of collecting information (data) from a primary source. It involves receiving information through any of the five senses, often with the aid of scientific instruments that extend the range of phenomena that can be observed (for example a microscope, a telescope, a radiation sensor and cameras) or that can take measurements (for example a tape measure, a measuring cylinder, a thermometer, a scale and a meter).
peer review	The process by which research is checked by experts in the same field to ensure that it meets the necessary standards of accuracy, reliability and validity before it is published. One reason that websites such as Wikipedia are not recommended as the sole source of information is that they have not been peer reviewed.

phenomenon	A fact, event, or situation that is observed to exist. The plural of phenomenon is phenomena.
precise	The precision of a measurement is its consistency, that is, the extent to which repeated measurements, taken under the same conditions, yield the same result. See also *reliable*.
premise	A starting statement or proposition from a conclusion inferred or deduced. In an 'if ... then ... ' statement, the premise is what follows 'if'.
references	Sources such as books, websites, and personal communications used to obtain information contained in a document. References are an important way of providing evidence. While the format, or style, of the reference information can vary, all references usually include the following information: author(s); date; title; and publication details.
reliable	1. A reliable *measurement* is one where repeated measurements, taken under the same conditions, yield the same result. See also *precise*. 2. A reliable *experiment* produces consistent results. Reliability is increased by repeating the experiment and averaging the results. 3. A *secondary source* is reliable if it can be substantiated by more than one reputable source.
signpost	To show the way to something. In a document, signposts provide cues and directions to readers to help them understand and navigate the document.
testable	A statement is testable if it can be determined whether it is true or false using experimentation or observation. A statement of opinion is not testable.
theory	A scientific theory is a well-substantiated and concise explanation of some natural phenomenon that is developed using valid scientific methods and repeatedly tested and confirmed through observation and experimentation. Scientific theories are based on fact, inductive in nature, and valued because they can accurately explain or predict phenomena.
valid	1. A valid *experiment* is a fair test. A method is valid if a) the procedure actually tests the hypothesis and the experiment includes an appropriate range of values; b) it uses appropriate equipment (for example, a measuring cylinder rather than a beaker to measure volume); c) variables are controlled; and d) appropriate measuring procedures are used.

2. A valid *measurement* is both accurate and precise.
3. A *secondary source* is valid if a) the author is qualified in the area; b) the article is unbiased; c) the publication is reputable; d) the data were gathered using appropriate methods and measuring devices; e) the source is recent; and f) the information relates to the hypothesis being investigated.

variable — Any factor or condition in an experiment that can be measured, controlled or changed. Variables can be of three types:

1. Independent variable is a condition that is changed by the experimenter. In a cause and effect situation, it is the cause.
2. Dependent variable is a condition that changes as a result of a change in the independent variable. In a cause and effect situation, it is the effect.
3. Controlled variable is a condition that does not change throughout the experiment. It is often used to compare the outcome of changes in other variables.

Note that many of these words have other meanings. The meanings in this glossary are those relevant to the contents of this book.

my notes

my notes

my notes

my notes

about the authors

Patricia Hipwell M.Ed., B.Sc. Econ. (Hons), Grad. Dip. of Literacy Ed., P.G.C.E., is an independent literacy consultant for her own company, **logonliteracy**. She delivers literacy professional development to teachers in Australia, and works predominantly in Queensland schools. Patricia has specialised in assisting all teachers to be literacy teachers, especially high school subject specialists who often struggle with what it means to be a content area teacher and a literacy teacher.

Malcolm Carter B.A. (Hons) P.G.C.E. M.A.C.E., operating through the business **Count on Numeracy**, is an independent consultant, providing professional development to teachers of science and mathematics throughout Australia. Malcolm has worked as a science teacher, Head of Science, Head of Curriculum and Principal for more than 40 years.

Merilyn (Lyn) Carter Ph.D., M.Ed.(Research), Dip.Ed., B.Ec., is also an independent consultant with **Count on Numeracy**, specialising in numeracy and mathematics. Her doctoral thesis investigated NAPLAN numeracy testing. Lyn also works as a researcher at the Queensland University of Technology (QUT).

Patricia and Lyn have created a number of resources to assist students' literacy and numeracy development. Patricia, Malcolm and Lyn are available (as a cross-curricular team or individually) to provide professional development in their areas of expertise and to support the use of their recommended resources, including this one.

For further information, contact:

Patricia Hipwell	Malcolm Carter	Lyn Carter
Mobile: 0429 727 313	Mobile: 0417 200 217	Mobile: 0402 077 958
pat.hipwell@gmail.com	countonnumeracy@bigpond.com	

logonliteracy

Count on Numeracy